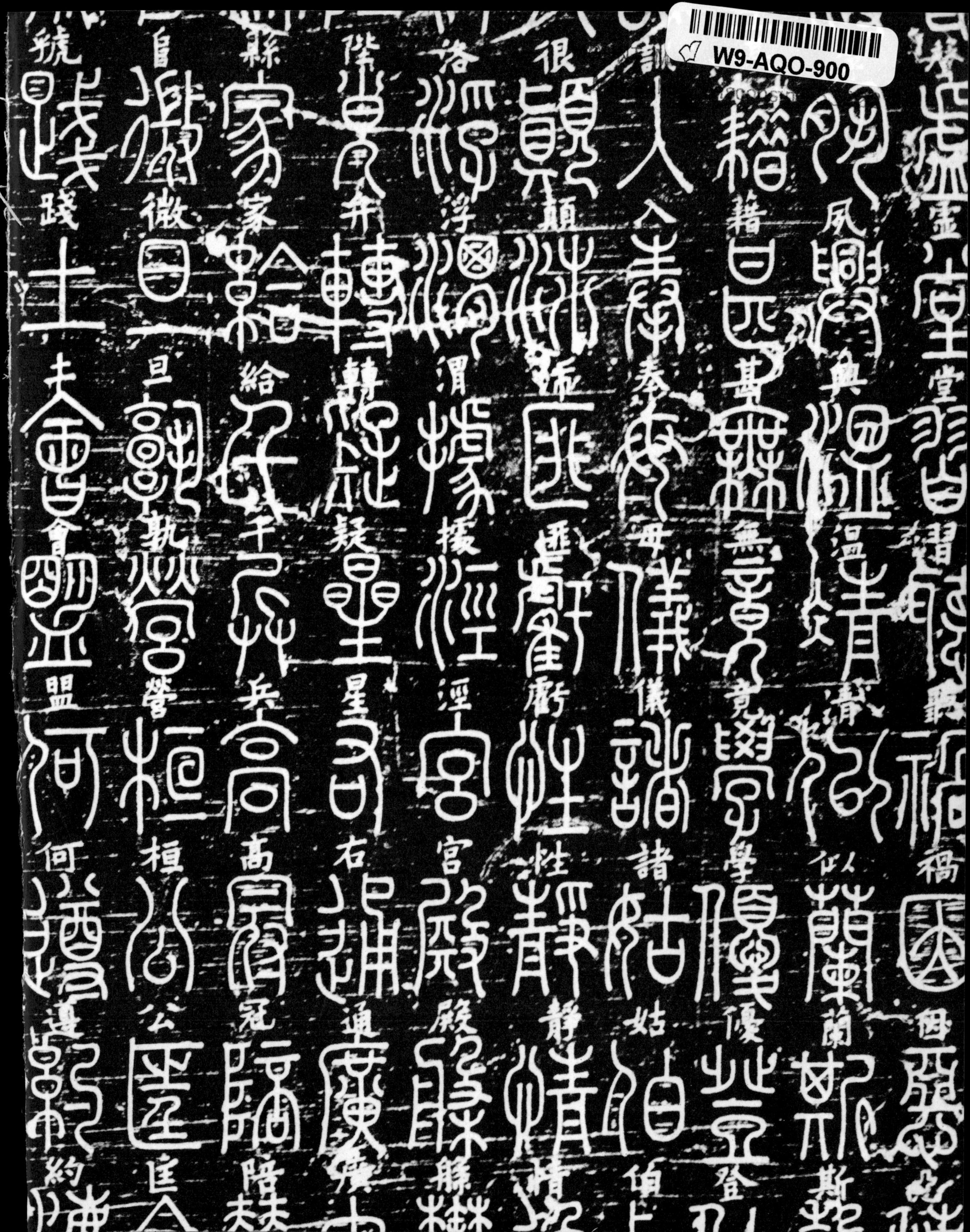

堂習聽禍
夙興溫凊似蘭
籍甚無竟學優登
奉母儀諸姑伯
顛沛匪虧性靜情
浮渭據涇宮殿
階弁轉疑星右通
縣家給千兵高冠陪
微旦孰營桓公匡
踐土會盟何遵約

to barbara and david

the
bann
of

marc riboud

the macmillan company / new york

three
ers
china

Library of Congress Catalog Card Number: 66–25644

First Printing

The Macmillan Company, New York
Collier Macmillan Canada Ltd., Toronto, Ontario

Printed in The Netherlands by Enschedé, Haarlem
Bound in The Netherlands by Jansen, Leiden

Things do not cease to exist, because we leave them behind.

Paul Claudel

In June 1965 I returned from a four months' journey to China. I had stayed there the same length of time in 1957, and I had remained obsessed with the desire to return and see again what I had seen once. I wanted to try and see more, and to see more clearly. Since my first journey, developments of considerable importance had taken place: the People's Communes, the Great Leap Forward, the new General Party Line—in short, what the Chinese call the three banners—which seemed to have transformed both China and world opinion on China.

Although France recognized China in 1964, as a French citizen I had to wait more than a year to obtain my visa. Just as in 1957, there was no lack of warnings before departure. "You will only see what the Chinese want to show you," I was told. "It will be a 'guided tour,' with the scenario prepared in advance." I was apprehensive about this. Everything might be colored by Peking's propaganda department and filtered through the medium of a conscientious guide. But I set out anyway, in the company of the journalist K. S. Karol, whose independent mind and critical sense could, no more than my own, tolerate a view through "rose-tinted spectacles."

It is certainly true that in China, as in all Communist countries, there is a different conception of journalism from our own. In China the journalist is duty-bound to present things as they ought to be rather than as they are. As we so often heard, he must be "positive." But, in spite of the polite attempts of some interpreters to win us over to this approach, we wanted to exercise our profession as we would have done in any country. This was not always an easy task. A European visitor does not travel in China the way he does in Europe or America. You cannot take a ticket and jump in a plane for Tibet or Sinkiang, or go by car from Peking to Shanghai. At a more basic level, you cannot pick up the phone and arrange your own meetings. All requests for travel outside Peking, as well as for visits and meetings, must go through the same official department. They are granted or refused, sometimes without apparent logic. On occasion visits are even suggested that you have not requested.

Were the interpreters a "shield" between us and reality? During our journey through the country a local interpreter was always waiting when we got off the train or plane. Much of the success of each stage depended upon him, and we had varied experiences. I recall that, when we visited the town of Chengchow, the capital of Honan, I wanted to stop the car in order to photograph an impressive vista of thousands of trees that had recently been planted along the avenues. The interpreter politely but firmly resisted. "No, not here," he said. "If you want to take pictures of trees, there are some in the courtyard of your hotel." Perhaps he thought it would be better if I indulged my "mania" in a safe and sheltered place. This was an exceptional case. By dint of polite insistence, patience, and diplomacy, we often in fact managed to see what we wanted, to go into houses that we chose, and even—though this was rare—to pay a random visit to a school or farm during a car journey through the countryside.

An interpreter accompanied us on all visits to such institutions as schools, factories, museums, and so on. Before the visit he took care to learn the appropriate technical terms. Usually his efforts were rewarded. Sometimes they were less so. Thus, when we were standing in front of the tomb of a Ming emperor, the interpreter pointed it out, saying: "Here in the middle is the emperor's tomb and, on either side, the small tombs of his two cucumbers." He meant "concubines." Did he miss a line in the dictionary, or was it his Chinese prudishness and shyness inhibiting him from uttering the latter word?

The interpreters, who were always young and sometimes just out of a university, often displayed an excessive modesty characteristic of the younger generation. During the showing of a very realistic movie on birth control, and in spite of the darkness which would have prevented us from seeing his blushes, our interpreter dared translate only the bare bones of the story, although our curiosity had been piqued by the laughter of the audience after certain passages in the commentary. Every time we asked male or female students about their plans for engagement or marriage, or about boy-girl relationships, and when we asked a young couple about birth control, the interpreter was as embarrassed and ashamed as those questioned. The only reply was an outburst of giggling which is, in the East, a polite and pleasant way of covering up embarrassment.

Did our interpreters show us only favorable aspects of China? In the first place, we were not always accompanied by a guide. In Peking and Shanghai we travelled around on our own, during the daytime and at night, without an interpreter. We went on foot, by taxi, or in a bus, just as we would have done in Rome or Tokyo. Our walks took us into the alleys of Peking's old quarter as well as into new industrial suburbs and housing estates. We entered restaurants, small shops, movie theatres, parks, deserted temples at will, without attracting any suspicion on the part of the local people, beyond that of some groups of children who were particularly amused by the length of our noses. These strolls around Peking and Shanghai were most revealing. They offered a wide, authentic panorama of Chinese reality.

In addition, we travelled more than 12,500 miles across China, from Harbin on the Siberian border to Nanning, which is not far from North Vietnam, crossing twelve of the eighteen Chinese provinces in the process. We accomplished most of the tour by train—Chinese trains, extremely punctual, go slowly enough to serve as an excellent observation platform.

The Chinese do not always show the best they have. They do not have qualms about arranging visits to enterprises which are no more than second-rate. Maybe this is done to show that they can "muddle through" in spite of everything. At Sian, in the heart of China, we asked, among other things, to visit some factories. On the last day two workshops were selected. In one, craftsmen were making basins and spittoons of enamelled metal and, in the other, shovels and pickaxes were being made by hand. We were ready to leave the great city of Sian, which has more than a million inhabitants, with a rather low impression of its level of industrialization. The plane was scheduled for the following day, but a storm prevented it from taking off and the next flight was twenty-four hours later. This left us a day to fill. Once more we asked if there were no other in-dustries in the city and our guide then carried us off to a factory making high-precision measuring and testing instruments, followed by another which manufactured machine-tools. Both employed more than 1,000 workers and were of praiseworthy modernity.

The best, and possibly the only, way of discovering China is to look at it. In every other country, human contacts help. In Algiers, Warsaw, San Francisco, Cuba, Moscow, etc., innumerable ex-changes and discussions with students, members of labor unions, and artists help one to complete and add definition to visual impressions. This is not possible in China. For the foreigner, even if he speaks Chinese, direct and spontaneous communication is practically non-existent. It is not only the language and the customs which are different. The thought process and the very reasons for living constitute additional screens masking the oriental façade. The replies you hear through the medium of the interpreter are usually ready-made formulas, recitals of the official viewpoint and the "correct attitude," and they are always dictated by the desire to follow the party line. One gets the impression that one could learn as much by translating *Jenmin Jihpao*, the Peking *People's Daily*. Dialogue as we know it, in which the personality of those talking comes across, is almost unknown. What do the Chinese think? What are their innermost concerns? How do they see the regime? We were told by some foreigners that even after several years of residence they could not answer these questions. The way officials try to vaunt the regime and extol its results sometimes ends in antagonizing the most sympathetic visitor. "Before the liberation," "After the liberation" become slogans as tedious as anything invented by Madison Avenue.

Thus, it is better to see, to look than to listen. A walk through the streets of Peking, across the rice paddies of Kwangsi, or the loess terraces of Shensi, able to record visually the unstudied gesture, the unguarded expression, was worth more than a dozen "explanations."

The first visual impression is that of poverty—an immense ocean of poverty. What is more, the Chinese make no attempt to conceal it. In the old sections of the big cities we saw houses crumbling with age, patched up with bits of wire and pieces of cardboard. We saw unpainted shopfronts corroded by time; unpaved streets; men and women wearing clothes which had been patched innumerable times.

In the countryside the picture is even more striking. Everywhere the dominant impression is one of obsolescence and erosion. There are the earth-colored houses with walls of dried mud and thatched roofs; faded clothes handed down from generation to generation; tools, utensils, and simple furnishings rusted, worn smooth, stained by years of wear and tear. It is as if everything had come from the depths of the past and had been handled by countless generations. The very countryside itself seems to be worn out. Trees have been torn up, roads and paths are more impressions left by millions of passers-by than routes laid out by the needs of the society.

This poverty is the heritage of a thousand years of history during which the average Chinese peasant and city-dweller had only one concern: individual survival. In fact, in spite of its ancient civilization, China, unlike European countries, has hardly ever possessed a real unity under central control, especially in recent times. This state of anarchy, as well as the virtually non-existent communications between the coasts and the interior, has contributed to keep the mass of the peasantry in conditions of the most extreme penury for centuries.

Age-old poverty, however, is at last in retreat. There is not much real destitution today. Even in the back alleys a considerable change is evident. The discipline of cleanliness is taking over. The slogan "cleanliness is an honor" seems to have passed into practice. There is no more refuse lying about, almost no flies or rats, no beggars at all. The brothels and opium dens have been closed. The food is spotlessly clean and we were able to eat and drink anywhere, even at little open-air stalls, without the slightest concern. This is rare in an Eastern country.

In spite of the increased population, there is a definite change in the overall situation. The new and the modern are gaining ground. I could not fail to notice the difference between my own two journeys of 1957 and 1965. Antiquated streetcars had been replaced by trolleybuses; avenues had been laid out; new schools, institutes, and hospitals had sprung up. Where there had been wasteland, new neighborhoods and factories had appeared. Despite its early fiascos the Great Leap Forward seems definitely to have brought about concrete facts, visible everywhere.

20. *The sedan-chair, detested symbol of the old China and its landowners and money-lenders, has not completely disappeared. But the only "privileged persons" who use it today are the sick and the old.*

In the countryside, where nine-tenths of the Chinese population live, progress is still barely visible. Here and there one finds an occasional tractor, bicycle, communal building, or power line. But the real change must be sought elsewhere, in a far-reaching transformation in the basic condition of the peasantry. In the old days the Chinese peasant was left to his own devices, subject to insecurity, the vagaries of the weather, the whims of the big landowner, and the law of the local overlord. There was no school. The cumulative centuries of poverty did not only have material consequences, but had plunged this mass of humanity into a self-sustaining vicious circle of illiteracy, ignorance, and superstition. No sense of community existed.

The device employed to awake this mass and to drag it out of its immemorial somnolence was the collective organization of the entire peasantry, the culmination of which is the People's Commune. We visited twenty communes, each one containing between 20,000 and 35,000 inhabitants and ranging from the banks of the Sungari in the far north-east, where the Siberian wind blows, to the deep, tropical south on the Burmese border, where posters urge the peasants to hand over the skins of the tigers they have killed to the authorities for a reward. In spite of distance and the problematical communications, we could see that the same system and structure were enforced everywhere. The commune is divided into brigades, which are in turn subdivided into teams of between twenty and thirty families. Each team is given a particular piece of land to cultivate, generally the same piece that its members and their ancestors have always farmed. The commune is an administrative unit, economically self-supporting. It does not depend on the state. Its profits are shared out among the workers according to the number of "labor grades" they have obtained and according to the total output of the team to which they belong. In the early euphoric days of the Revolution, the authorities envisaged implementing the slogan of the "ten freedoms": free food, clothing, housing, schooling, medical services, heating, leisure activities, hairdressing, marriage, and burial. Today the ten freedoms have become the "five guarantees," the first five on the list. The small salaries that the peasants receive cover the rest.

In 1958 there were also local attempts to institute communal meals, but they were soon abandoned. Everywhere, in fact, the family remains the basic unit of everyday life, whether it is a question of feeding, housing, or work. The same house usually provides shelter for three generations, and the poultry, the pig, and a small plot of land also remain family property. Some heads proudly list the new, personal acquisitions of individual members of their communes as a sign of improvement in the general standard of living. For example, in the October First Commune near Nanking, which numbers 24,000 inhabitants, bicycles have increased in five years from 180 to 847, alarm-clocks from 450 to 1,821, and wrist-watches from zero to 70. Everywhere we noticed that the leaders of the teams and brigades worked side by side with the other peasants, that the leadership always came from the village or region, and that there seemed to be a kind of grass-roots democracy in the form of meetings and frequent discussions at which everyone was encouraged to express his opinions and criticisms. Traditional village rivalries, we were told, now served the purpose of stimulating competition between teams and brigades.

The commune heads did not disguise the fact that the amounts of agricultural machinery and fertilizer were still very inadequate. Their great pride was irrigation. We could see with our own eyes how the many little channels and reservoirs have changed the face of the Chinese plain. They have enabled the peasants to combat natural calamities and were described everywhere as the "decisive factor" which has enabled famine to be defeated. The French agricultural economist René Dumont has said that "this attempt at irrigating the land is by far the greatest which has ever been achieved in this sphere by any country in history." Similarly, the planting of millions of trees has begun to alter the face of the hills and mountains.

Not since Emperor Shih Wang-ti dug the great canal in the north in the second century B.C. has a government so concerned itself with the future as to organize and carry out such vast enterprises. It does seem that it is the discipline and collective effort of the communes which made it possible. The peasant of old China had to live selfishly and for the moment to survive. Why should he dig canals for irrigation? They would have benefited his neighbor. Why should he want to plant trees? He was more likely to have torn them up for fire wood. Thus the People's Communes are in the process not only of changing the face of the land, but of reshaping the mentality of the man who works it.

Text continued on page 65

1 the people's communes

25. *The People's Communes have brought enormous changes in the life of the Chinese peasants. But they have not altered, and possibly will not alter for some time, the basic movements or age-old implements of these two peasant women from the south.*

26. *In contrast to Lenin, Mao, who was of peasant stock, based the Chinese Revolution on the peasantry. He was born in Shao Shan in the heart of China into a family of small landholders. Today, his house (below) is a place of pilgrimage. Young Mao learned to swim in the pond. The village has become a model commune. The plastic sheets are to protect the rice plants from frost.*

27 *(above). Here is the room where Mao spent his childhood. The earth floor, dried-mud walls, and simple furniture are explained to visitors as examples of the austerity which must shape the new generation.*

27 *(below). On the other side of the pond, a peasant family still lives in similar conditions. The bed, with its mosquito-net, is like Mao's. This old peasant woman saw Mao born and grow up. Her daughter still spins at the spinning-wheel. Since he came to power, Mao has returned once to his village.*

28. *Mao Tse-tung's bed in Yennan. After the Long March in the 1930s the Chinese Communists hid in these caves in the cliff face. They lived here for more than ten years, formulating their doctrine. The men who even today are responsible for China's policy were schooled here under rigorous conditions. "A mosquito-net was the most luxurious thing I possessed in Yennan,"* Mao has said.

29. *The head of the People's Commune of Shao Shan, Mao's native village, is respon-* sible for 10,720 peasants. He is also called Mao. With his hand on the customary glass of tea, he tells with pride of having known Chairman Mao in his youth.

30-31. *This old peasant couple were not expecting a visit from a foreigner. Jars of soya, thermos flasks, ropes, and matting form the familiar background against which they have spent their lives. The only picture on the wall is a family portrait. The People's Commune has guaranteed them regular food and electric light.*

32 *(above). These two tractors are of Chinese make. They are harrowing the paddy-fields near Nanning. The commune has twelve machines for a cultivated area of some 3,000 acres. One still sees few tractors in the Chinese countryside.*

32 *(below). Large numbers are still the commonest substitute for mechanization. In a small, thatched-roof village in Yünnan, part of a team of Sanyis women work in tight formation. The team is the smallest production unit of the commune.*

33. *This peasant woman from the Peking area cherishes the vase, oil-lamp, clock, and mirror which she inherited from her parents. On the chest, near the radio, the thermos flask always contains the hot water which is traditionally offered to visitors as "white tea." On the wall, one of the posters carries the slogan: "Let us ardently love Chairman Mao; let us ardently love the Communist Party."*

34-35. *Labor in the paddy-fields of Kwangsi is now a collective effort. The buffaloes belong to the commune. There is never any lack of rain in this area and there are often two harvests a year.*

36. *This old lady belongs to the Sanyis racial minority in Yünnan. She does not speak Chinese, but her daughter is learning to read and write Mandarin at the commune school. National minorities form 6 per cent of China's population.*

37. *Chinese painters did not take the strange shapes of their landscapes from their imagination. They painted the extravagant contours of these mountains in Kuelin from life. The rice planters are used to this spectacular scenery.*

38-39. *All the way along the Yellow River, the loess, which is a very good soil for wheat, is cut into terraces. Each year, 12 million more Chinese must be fed and, in order to obtain arable land, the peasants make new terraces in these mountains every year, sometimes on the edge of great precipices.*

40. *This old peasant woman leaning on her elbows beside the Yangtze wears the jacket, patched countless times, which she has worn all her life. "To be clean is an honor", says the slogan, but to wear old clothes is also considered a badge of honor. One frequently sees technicians and even high-ranking managers wearing patched clothes.*

41. *(above). These two young farmers are returning from the market. The new bicycle, the good quality clothes, and the Western-style umbrella are still a rare sight and were unheard of ten years ago. They are signs of the slow but sure improvement in the peasant's standard of living. This photograph was taken in a commune of Yünnan province.*

41 *(below). On the way to market, where they are going to sell the pig. Each peasant family has the right to cultivate its private plot of land and to raise a few domestic animals. This is a vital contribution to the family budget.*

42-43. *In the north, near Loyang, the soil is dry. Rain is eagerly awaited. On the left, a channel has been dug for irrigation. At plowing time the schoolchildren come and help the peasants, removing stones and weeds. This is part of Maoist doctrine: Work must form part of education.*

44. *It used to be said that the transplanting of rice could never be mechanized. At Nanning, in the south, engineers have perfected a semi-automatic machine which spares women the tiring work of transplantation. As yet these machines are being turned out only in small numbers, but the Chinese are proud of having exported a few to Africa.*

45. *A team of about sixty workers is the basic unit of the People's Commune. In order to clear new ground, this team is working side by side. In the midst of them is their leader, who is not supposed to be set apart from the other farmers. Today China has about 268 million acres under cultivation, and she hopes to double this area.*

46-47. *In May, in the far north, near the Siberian border, the weather is severe. The peasants have padded coats and the women wear headscarves. Teamwork is the rule for the transplantation of plants and watering.*

48-49. *Policymakers quickly gave up the idea of making the communal experiment all-embracing. These southern peasants eat rice, vegetables, and occasionally a little pork in their homes with the rest of their families. Only the workers attached to the commune's central administration must eat in the canteen.*

50. *This female agricultural laborer works on a state farm. With her chopsticks still in her hand, she is leaving the canteen and is reading* China Youth. *The big headline reads: "Successful explosion of second Chinese atomic bomb." The second headline reads: "Three million demonstrators parade in support of the Dominican Republic." In order to read a newspaper, you need to know 3,000-4,000 characters.*

51 *(above). In the old days, glasses were the hallmark of those who could read and write. This peasant is still wearing the large, round spectacles his grandfather left him.*

51 *(below). A tremendous literacy campaign has been carried out in China. In every commune, evening classes were established at which peasants, young and old, learned to read and write.*

52. *It is the first time these peasants from Langchow have sat on school benches. Fifteen years ago, 80 per cent of the population was illiterate.*

53. *These two peasants come from Shensi in the north. One of their old provincial proverbs said: "A poor man has no right to speak." They are going to evening classes and are starting to read.*

54-55. *At nightfall, a team of young peasant women return from the fields. They look like the young factory girls who are leaving the factory. Like them, they average eight hours a day, although the hours vary with the seasons and local needs.*

56. *This peasant woman in a suburban train in Canton is in a "soft" compartment. The other compartments are "hard." No permit is needed for Chinese to travel inside the country, but foreigners must have a travel permit in order to board the train. Music, which takes on a triumphal rhythm at each arrival and departure, and various items of news, are broadcast over loudspeakers in each compartment, although the volume can be controlled.*

57. *Langchow, the gateway to the distant province of Sinkiang, in 1957. Entire families of peasants, with all their belongings, get off the trains coming from the east.*

58. *China still has very few trucks and tractors. In many areas draught animals are scarce. You still see carts drawn by men and women, young and old alike. In order to make the task easier, the wheels have been fitted with tires.*

59. *In Chungking, by the side of the Yangtze, human effort is still used to tow the boats. This city of three million people has only recently been linked to the coast by railroad. Before, all transport was by river.*

60. *Just as everywhere else in the east, the peasant women take their children with them to the fields.*

61. *Rural electrification is one of the régime's main objectives. Even today the vast majority of villages is without electricity. The communes are in charge of the erection of power lines on their territory. With makeshift equipment, a team of youngsters puts up the poles. Soon the current will light their homes.*

62-63. *Chungking, the capital of Szechwan and rice bowl of China, built on the banks of the Yangtze, was the refuge of Chiang Kai-shek during the Sino-Japanese war.*

Finally, in every village, there is a school, for which the commune is responsible. Whether it is installed in a deserted temple, the former landowner's house, or the only new building in the village, it has pride of place. We saw children who had never been to school learn not only how to read and write, but also how to observe rules of hygiene and "social ethics." In spite of the existence of innumerable dialects, it is Pei-hua, the language of Peking, which, with that ever-present basic concern for unity, is taught throughout the huge country. From an early age civic and political "education" is combined with academic work. With the aid of detailed examples, children are shown the conditions in which their parents lived and are told that the advantages they now enjoy are due to the Revolution. Moreover, schools are not only for children. Adults are to be found there in the evenings. It is a moving sight to see the wrinkled features of old peasants emerging from a lifetime's apathy to stammer out a few of the thousands of Chinese characters.

So that we could appreciate the Great Leap Forward, we were constantly reminded of the point from which China started out in 1949. After years of anarchy, civil war, and foreign occupation, it was virtually zero. There was no real industry. The yardstick was the production of steel: 150,000 metric tons. (Today West Germany produces 36 million metric tons annually.) The only industrial center, Manchuria, had been almost entirely stripped by the Russians following the departure of the Japanese. From 1954 onwards the take-off began with Russian help, but in 1960 the sudden recall of Soviet experts nearly precipitated a catastrophe. Overnight China found herself deprived of all foreign aid and this led to years of crisis, necessitating a period of so-called readjustment. It was then that the slogan "Let us rely on our own strength" was coined; it can still be seen on all suburban walls as well as in factories and institutes. These years taught the Chinese to rely on their own inventive genius, patience, and determination. As a result of their ingenuity, they are now capable of producing everything which defines a modern industrial economy: electronic brains, transistors, microscopes, high-precision machine-tools, and even, alas, the Bomb. But when we visited the factories, and were able to verify this capacity to produce something of everything, we were also able to see that China was still a long way from using the assembly-line or mass-production techniques that alone could satisfy the needs of 700 million people—a population greater than that of the USA, the USSR, and Europe combined.

The two or three isolated factories we saw employing assembly-line methods—trucks at Shangchung or tractors at Loyang—had been built entirely by the Russians. It also seemed to us that there was a disproportionately large number of workers at the machines for a relatively limited output. But for the moment the watchword is "diversity and quality." The Chinese have not yet reached the level of technical proficiency necessary for the perfection of automated machines.

It is mainly in order to make up this lag, and to jump such a large population in one leap across the enormous gap separating China from the twentieth century, that the authorities impose their extremely rigorous discipline. The Chinese way of life today is very austere. There is no individual liberty in the sense that we understand it. The authorities wish to waste no energy; it must all be harnessed in the same way, to the same objectives. Although he is sure not to be unemployed, the student leaving a university or technical college cannot choose the factory where he is to work or even the place where he is to live. Students invariably replied to our question, "What will you do and where will you work when you have completed your studies?" with, "We shall go wherever our country needs us."

Unmarried workers in newly built factories sleep in nearby barracks, but we also saw cases of married men separated from their wives in the "interests of the economy." Usually it was a case of young technicians or engineers whose wives worked in another area. They would meet once a week. But in one Peking factory, a young worker we questioned told us that her husband was a soldier and that she had seen him only once a year for several years. A similar situation could arise with a teacher or a civil servant. When we asked about the absence of freedom of choice in jobs and the conditions of family life, one official replied, "Do you think those hundreds of thousands of men who live and sleep in the streets of Bombay and Calcutta and who are, for the most part, separated from their families, are more free?" We Westerners mention frequently "freedom of choice" as an ideal, yet real freedom of choice operates in only a small part of the world; elsewhere it is economical conditions that dictate or limit the choice. *Text continued on page 133*

2 the great leap forward

69. *The Great Leap Forward was designed to thrust China into the twentieth century. But the distance which has to be spanned is considerable. For the Leap to succeed, 120 million Chinese children must first go to school. This poor, isolated village in Kwangsi in the south used to have no school. Today, before going into the classroom, the children listen to a lesson in patriotism from the teacher.*

70-71. *In the nursery at textile factory No. 2 in Peking, little Chinese are taught that the world is made up of children of all colors.*

72-73. *"Make your own wooden rifles!" is the injunction to boys and girls of the Young Pioneer movement. To develop discipline, they are taught to march in step. The Chinese children still hanging around the streets are fascinated by the Pioneers.*

74. *The taste for experiment is fostered at an early age. This fourteen-year-old school-girl is examining a piece of tissue under a "made in China" microscope.*

75. *An anatomy lesson in a secondary school. The topmost character on the display card means "heart." A plastic demonstration model, which can be taken apart, is beside the teacher. In groups of three, the children will dissect an animal's heart.*

76. *At the age of ten, the children of this primary school from a commune in Honan can already read several thousand characters. The Chinese script comprises several tens of thousands, but the government has launched a program to simplify them and reduce their number.*

77. *Everywhere in the new China the young people are passionately keen to read and to learn. The University of Peking has 12,000 students. Tuition is free.*

78-79. *This dormitory, where seven female students of the university of Kunming are spending four years studying, is as bare as a convent cell. The bed consists of a thin piece of matting upon a narrow frame, together with a mosquito-net. On the shelf there are some books, including the works of Mao. On the wall there is a picture of Lenin and the five rules for "model dormitory behavior." Most of the students are of peasant and working-class stock. Austere and disciplined though it is, university life seems like luxury to these peasants' daughters.*

80. *A student's satchel on a library table. He has chosen a classical image of the Chinese female with which to cover one of his books. Even in austere conditions, dreams have their place.*

81. *Three-quarters of the students are oriented toward science and technology. Scientific education has become one of the most repeated themes of political slogans: "Let us support the three great revolutionary movements: class struggle, battle for production, and scientific progress."*

82 *(above). Mao proclaims physical education a national necessity. Every day, throughout the country, workers, public employees, clerks, and students do physical training between 10 and 10:10 in the morning. It is impossible for the foreigner to remain unimpressed. There is now something different about the physical appearance of young Chinese.*

82 *(below). The new régime has opened a Western-style ballet school in Peking, but these young ballerinas will appear only in ballets on revolutionary themes. Like other students, they are working in a commune or factory one month a year.*

83. *"Peking man" was the ancestor of the Chinese. He lived in a cave, 400,000 years ago. Geology students are told that the stone and bone tools found near the skeleton support the Marxist thesis that "work makes man." Archaeological excavations are being carried out all over the country.*

84-85. *As soon as they can read, children in Peking rent comic books in the street for a few cents. These tell of exploits of heroes in the national and revolutionary struggle, but sometimes also illustrate poetic stories of traditional folklore.*

86-87. *A Ching lion, a Czech bus, Western-style umbrellas, and Chinese parasols go to make up this Peking street scene. A primary school is letting out.*

88. *An unusual sight, which you could no longer see today. On a Peking street, an aristocrat, wrapped in her indifference, passes like a stranger through a world which she no longer recognizes. This picture was taken in 1957.*

89. *The Bridge of Heaven in Peking's suburbs is the place where traditional popular amusements draw crowds on Sundays. Even on weekdays there are plenty of idlers around watching.*

90-91. *"Art and Craft Export Company. We buy diamonds, emeralds, pearls, precious stones, carpets, embroidery, china, etc. ...Open as usual." Thus reads the sign outside this shop, whose gold-lettered name means "Prosperity." Private citizens come here to sell family jewels or other objects. The prices are fixed by the government. This scene has been photographed in old Peking through the window of a shop on Liu Li Chang, the street long famous for its art and antique shops.*

92. *These working-class girls, assembling transistors, earn the same wages (about $20 a month) as those in Canton or Nanking, but they are distinctive for their elegance. They come from Shanghai.*

93. *Czech trolleybusses and Chinese busses have replaced the antiquated streetcars which were still in service a few years ago in the streets of Peking. A bus ride costs 11 fen (5 cents). Pedicabs still often carry goods and occasionally passengers. Here they transport new empty trunks coming out of a workshop. Rickshaws have disappeared all over China and most able-*

94-95. *A bicycle costs about $70 or three times the average monthly pay check. Their number is increasing all the time and they represent, especially in the towns, the first sign of an improvement in the standard of living. They are left in the streets without padlocks, as here outside a movie theatre. Each one carries a registration number.*

96-97. *The first bridge over the Yangtze. With its eight piers and its length of nearly 2,000 yards, it is the largest bridge in Asia. In 1957 it was in the course of construction. Soviet engineers helped to design and build it; it cost $60 million. At Hankow it*

98. In old Manchuria, the Anshan steel-works are China's Ruhr, its greatest industrial complex. Some of the 15,000 workers leave work.

99. At the entrance to a machine-tool and ball-bearing factory in Kunming (Yünnan), a large signboard illustrates the Great Leap Forward. It was painted by one of the factory workers.

100-101. *This truck factory was built entirely by the Soviets in 1955. The 30,000 workers and engineers it now employs are all Chinese and all very young. Like everywhere else, there are slogans. This one says: "Let us make one more step forward in our political ideology."*

100

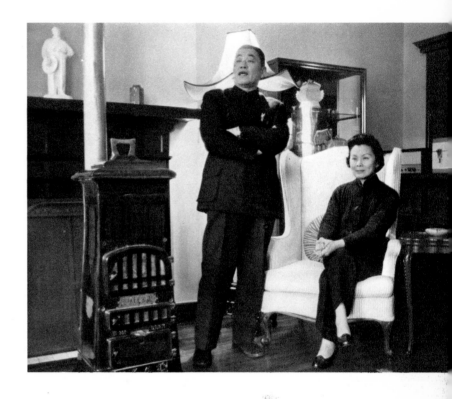

102. *The control-room of several blast-furnaces at Anshan. Above the control-panel, the banners of the best teams are on display. One reads: "Let us develop the revolutionary spirit in order to attain the summit of technology." The technicians are indistinguishable from the workers.*

103. *Mr. Lou Lei-i is a "national capitalist." He belongs to a rich Shanghai industrial family, most of whose members emigrated. He chose to stay. His factories were taken over by the state, but he receives 5 per cent of their value as estimated by the government. Appointed director of one of them, he is also a member of the National Consultative Assembly and vice-president of the Shanghai Chamber. He has kept his comfortable house, and has added Mao's bust to the mantlepiece.*

104. *In his office is the manager of a 3,000-man factory in Shanghai, which makes small three-wheeled trucks. He earns the equivalent of $60 a month, which is twice as much as an unskilled worker but hardly any more than a skilled worker or engineer. The three slogans on the unpainted wall are: "A fighting and stubborn spirit; ardent class feeling; a rigorous scientific attitude."*

105. *A young working-girl from Shanghai. Everywhere women work in factories and earn the same wages as men. They are employed wherever their dexterity can be useful, but they are also seen working heavy machine-tools and cranes.*

106. *In an engineering workshop in Nanking, the leaping horses with the exaggerated eyebrows symbolize the Great Leap Forward. It is the most common symbol in factories. The riders are workers.*

107. *Three factories make tractors. This one at Loyang, built by the Russians in 1955, is by far the most important and is the only one which uses assembly-line methods. It employs 20,000 workers and turns out fifty Soviet World War II-model tractors a day. Each one carries the words "The East Is Red" in gold letters.*

108-109. *These workers on the engine assembly-line at the same factory come, for the most part, from peasant families in the area. They are very young and were trained on the job at the factory's school.*

110-111. *Foreigners are not allowed to visit oil refineries. At Harbin, not far from the Siberian border, a large, recently built factory manufactures storage-tanks and pipelines for the refineries.*

112. *Acoustic testing of valves on the engine test-bench at the truck works in Ch'ang Ch'ung. Many skilled workers and technicians from this factory spent some time in the Soviet Union between 1956 and 1960; they speak Russian. The greater part of the material in the factory's technical library is in Russian. Three- to four-month-old American and European technical journals can also be found as well as American technical books translated into Russian.*

113. *This three-wheeled-truck factory in Shanghai, built by the Chinese, is equipped for the most part with Chinese machinery. As it does not employ assembly-line methods, it turns out only five trucks a day. The tires are also of Chinese make.*

114-15. *No longer half-starved coolies, but twentieth-century workers, are making coke in the new eastern suburb of Peking.*

116. *The number of miles of railroad, which was less than 12,500 in 1949, has now more than doubled. But it is still too small for the country's needs. This Anshan rolling-mill, built by the Soviets in Manchuria, is the only one which makes rails.*

117. *This is not a clock, but the automatic control-panel of the rolling-mill. Manchuria was industrialized by the Japanese and a*

working class already existed in the region. The average age of the workers is higher than in areas more recently industrialized.

118-19. *Twenty-four years old and un-married, she is from the Steel Institute in Peking. She sleeps in barracks near the factory and earns $34 a month. To eat her bowl of rice, she has simply lifted up her goggles. Her canteen meal costs 20 cents.*

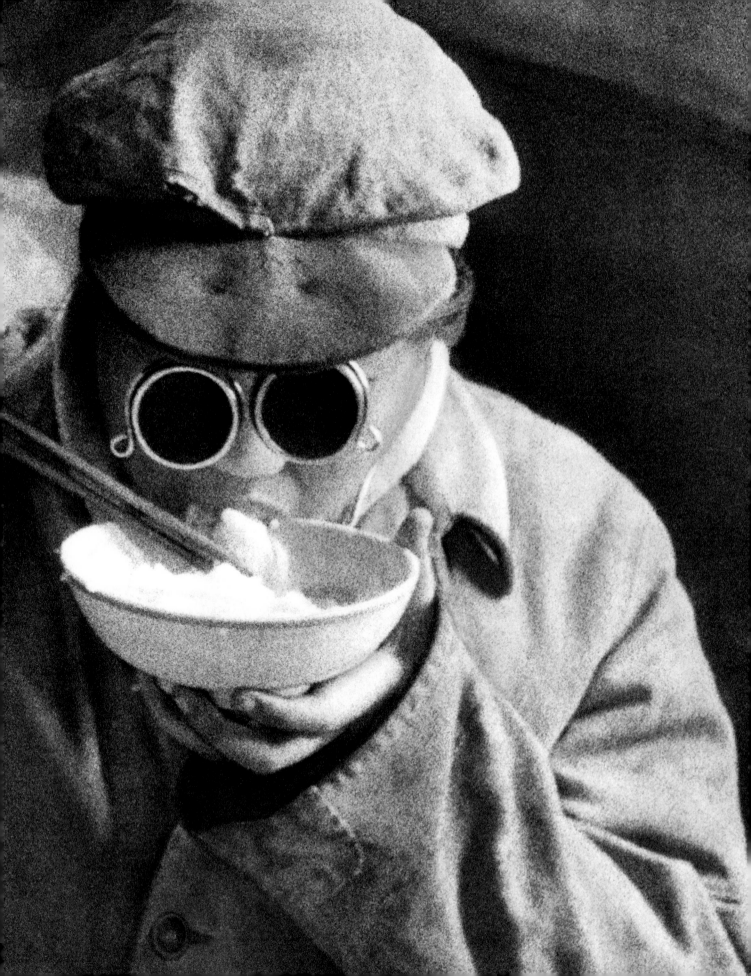

120. *In 1957 many posters called for good relations with the Soviet experts. "Let us actively learn to draw lessons from the progressive experience of the Soviet Union," said this one at Wuhan. In 1960 Krushchev withdrew the 1,390 Russian experts and you now read on the posters: "Let us rely solely upon our own strength."*

121. *Advertisements have disappeared from the streets of Shanghai and great signboards now seek to inform and educate consumers. This one boasts about "Pure woollen items, in color, which keep their warmth and are long-lasting. We make four kinds."*

122. *Movie advertisements are huge, painted signboards. This one depicts a scene from the resistance against the Japanese invader. Most movies have a patriotic or political purpose. Actors, like artists and writers, earn no more than an engineer. Also, like everyone else, they have to spend a month a year working in a factory or People's Commune.*

123. *In a large Canton store on the eve of the Chinese New Year, there is a crowd round the toy counter. All the toys are made in China. The assistants are students; they are carrying out their compulsory weekly day at work. Shops are open on Sundays and holidays. In all towns, there is at least one large department store, state-owned and selling everything from shaving cream to pianos, all Chinese-made. Small shops are half-state, half privately owned. The prices are fixed by the government.*

124. *At Kunming, as in all provincial capitals, a permanent fair displays the local products. On this stand are the fabrics and clothes made in the new textile factory nearby. Although a spectacular effort has been made in the field of textiles, a lot of time is needed before all 700 million Chinese will have new clothes.*

125. *Evening falls on Changan, the large avenue in Peking. In March it is still cold*

and the non-com (right) has on his fur hat. In June 1965 insignia of rank were abolished in the Chinese army.

126-27. *Six a.m. in the great central market in Shanghai. It is the rush hour. In the foreground they are selling dried eels at 0.45 yuan (20 cents) a pound. Vegetables are plentiful. Between 1960 and 1963 there was a serious food shortage in China, but the position greatly improved in 1965.*

北 京 一 特·快 一 广 州
BEIJING   TEKUAI   GUANGZHOU

128. *In Peking there are restaurants catering to all tastes. This one, in a downtown section, is Mongol. With the help of chopsticks people are cooking their own small slices of mutton in a communal receptacle divided into compartments. Burning coals keep the water boiling. The two-yuan note (80 cents) is good for three meals. Like the majority of restaurants, it is a mixed enterprise (part privately owned and part state-owned). The official guide to Peking lists thirty good restaurants, where both service and food are first class. A good meal can comprise twelve courses or more, and ends with soup. Beer, sweet wine, or rice alcohol is drunk with the meal.*

129. *1,440 miles separate Peking (Beijin) from Canton (Guangzhou). Beijing and Guangzhou are the romanized Chinese phonetic transcriptions of the characters. It takes forty-six hours for the express (Tekuai) to link the two cities. Staff sell travelers tea bags and regularly top up glasses and cups with hot water. The trains are slow but punctual, and very clean.*

130-31. *In Canton on Chinese New Year everyone is in the streets. Bamboo stands have been erected by the suburban communes to display and sell their prettiest flowers. It is like carnival time and loudspeakers broadcast slogans and march music.*

132. *With its seven million inhabitants, Shanghai is the third largest city in the world. On Sundays the inhabitants like to go for strolls in the streets. The stores remain open. Everywhere, on the walls, there are educational slogans. The one in the background says: "Get in the habit of not spitting on the ground at random."*

In short, the Peking regime sees this choice: anarchic freedom, which in overpopulated and underdeveloped countries engulfs the weakest and poorest in physical and moral misery; or Spartan egalitarianism and quasi-military discipline, which improves the standard of living and gives the masses "a sense of order and dignity."

The excesses to which anarchic individualism led the Chinese in the past—corruption, prostitution, gambling, opium smoking, etc.—perhaps explain the present-day excess in the opposite direction, towards compulsive puritanism. Nothing is more shocking, for example, than the sentence of death upon a teacher we saw posted outside a People's Court in Kueilin (see page 177). The mixture of moral and political sermonizing is disturbing; it must also be doubted that all the violated young pupils were entirely unwilling accomplices. But we must also try to understand that the general depravity of old China, the legacy of years of civil war, and the Japanese occupation could not vanish in a few years. Assaults upon young people are severely punished in all countries, more so in China because it was in crimes such as these that the old regime was worst. The theatre, literature, and, indeed, all the arts are victims of the wave of puritanism. Not only have all erotic themes been banned, but even sentimental ones, as well as all references to personal happiness. In both form and content, contemporary Chinese art is hopelessly conventional. The country which saw the rise of Tang sculpture and Sung painting produces nothing nowadays above the level of the mediocre. The watchword is: "Art in the service of the Revolution."

The Chinese leaders believe in man's perfectibility. They want to build a new kind of man, man who will no longer be inspired by self-interest, the profit motive, or personal prestige, but by the common good, self-denial, integrity, and the desire to pursue the Revolution. Ideally the regime wants to bring about this transformation not by force or punishment, except in a few special cases, but by persuasion, example, and conditioning. And, so far as we were able to see, integrity, honesty, and the community spirit were gaining ground in China, by a process of contagious example—just as corruption and inertia spread by contagious example in old China.

There is no better analogy to the way of life imposed upon young Chinese than the rules of a monastic order. There is the same moral rigor, the same austerity, the same preaching of chastity, obedience, help to others. The example held out to young Chinese is the soldier Lei Feng, who was killed in an ordinary truck accident. There was nothing remarkable about his life, no outstanding act of gallantry. Above all else he was well disciplined; he carried out his duties perfectly and in obscurity. He told children stories, helped old people across the road, lent a helping hand to his comrades on the construction site, was careful with the gas for his truck, mended his own socks, and so on. Finally, most important of all, he read Mao Tse-tung's works every day. The movie depicting his life is shown everywhere. We found it painfully naïve and were saddened to see even Peking university students eating it up. But we had forgotten that the majority of these students are the sons and daughters of peasants: in some respects, their mental age is no more than thirteen or fourteen. As children of this age, they need to be taught everything about life in a community. We were able to see just how much the Chinese needed this kind of lesson on several occasions. One day I was walking in Liu Li-chang, a mean street in the old quarter of Peking which is always crowded. A man of over fifty, no doubt a worker, was returning home on his ancient bicycle. He was pedalling slowly and with difficulty. All of a sudden his front fork broke and he fell face down on the road. The men and women walking along this narrow street neither turned back nor stopped; they simply moved to avoid him. Nobody helped the old man. He got up on his own, his mouth covered with blood. Such indifference was the hallmark of the old China. If there had been a youngster there, perhaps he would have followed the example of Lei Feng, learned at school. Perhaps not. But if the Chinese everywhere are being repeatedly told, by means of movies and slogans, to help one another, it is because they are no longer aware of this rule of life in society and have to be retaught it.

Chinese Communism is a secular religion. Its Bible is the works of Mao Tse-tung. A good Chinese, a good Communist, must read Mao every day. He is continually told that he can find in Mao the solutions to his simple every-day problems. On several occasions, when we were visiting a workshop or a construction site, the foreman told us that it had been possible to overcome technical difficulties thanks to correct application of Chairman Mao's thinking, whether it was a question of manufacturing ball-bearings or road-building. The Chinese victor in the world table-tennis championships said in an interview in the *People's Daily* that he had won because he had applied the tactics learned from Mao's works: find the enemy's weak spot and concentrate your entire strength against it.

Mao's central idea is to avoid, at all costs, the formation of a new class. Today, economic advancement, especially in the towns, might conceivably enable the technicians, engineers, and administrators to improve their standard of living to the degree where they could separate from the poorer sections of the community. Mao and his fellow leaders believe that, if they allow this tendency to develop, future economic development will itself be compromised, as well as the purity of Communism. They consider that if a minority improves its standard of living there is a danger that it will become increasingly bourgeois; it will then become much more difficult to improve standards for the masses. The amount of improvement remaining to be done is so enormous that the regime will not permit any relaxation or waste of effort. The struggle against the recrudescence of individualism is called the "struggle against modern revisionism." Everything is done to avoid this development. Students, clerks, technicians, factory managers, artists, and party officials are dispatched to communes and factories for one day a week and one month a year. Some spend a full year in a commune. The authorities told us that they were aware of the loss of output which such constant shifting entailed, but they felt that in the long run it would be advantageous for the country's economic and political future, as well as for the unity of the Chinese people.

In the same spirit, everything is done so that the Chinese, and particularly the younger generation, are not contaminated by contacts with foreigners with standards of living superior to their own. This attitude was clearly expressed in a recent editorial in the Peking *People's Daily*, which declared in a comment upon an American request for an exchange of journalists that "Washington officials were indulging in day-dreams if they were speculating on the possibility of undermining the militant ardor of the Chinese people and, in particular, of the younger generation by means of the process of evolution encouraged by contact with the United States." This forced austerity, perpetuated at all costs, may seem futile and inhuman to us, but it is seen by the regime as the *sine qua non* of a slow but general improvement in the conditions of the vast, poverty-stricken masses. China wants a society in which individual material recompense is absent; to allow contact with the society in which material recompense is the basis of its system must seem to them the most dangerous and compromising thing.

People have spoken of the "Yenan complex" of the Chinese. Yenan was that terribly harsh and austere place of refuge where the majority of the present leadership spent ten years of their lives after the Long March. It has been said that, cut off from the rest of the world behind self-erected walls, they judge both Chinese and international affairs with a "poverty" complex. This is probably true. But we Westerners may also be surrounded by high walls in a closed world of "prosperity" which prevents us from seeing and understanding the other world.

Text continued on page 206

3 the general party line

139. *The Party is everything. It is the Party which formulates the General Line, the basis of the doctrine which dictates social organization, and the life of the lowliest citizen. The Party is the group of leaders whose portraits are on sale in all the big stores. At the top there is Mao Tse-tung, and immediately below four of the members of the Political Bureau: Liu Shao-chi, Chou En-lai, Chu Teh, Chen Yi. Lenin and Stalin are also honored.*

140-41. *At the Steel Institute in Peking, political courses start with everyone chanting: "Socialism is good!"*

142. *The administrative office of a large Peking factory. The furniture is very simple. Beneath the glass top of his desk a clerk has inserted some family photographs, Chinese and Malaysian stamps, a calendar, and a Russian portrait of Lenin.*

143. *A Marxist-Leninist seminar for budding engineers at the Geological Institute. Like all students, they have three hours a week set aside for political courses or discussions.*

144. *To increase productivity, the names and portraits of deserving workers are posted up at the factory gates. The authorities have largely abolished the profit motive, trying to replace it with "socialist emulation." However, bonuses are sometimes awarded, although they are small and form less than 10 per cent of the pay check.*

145. *Like advertisements, slogans must catch the eye. With different chalks, a workman has written on a factory blackboard: "Let us hold high the banner of Mao Tse-tung. Let us achieve the resolutions adopted by the assembly of deputies and workers. Let us develop the revolutionary* spirit. Let us realize the coordination of labor. Let us ensure security and let us realize the seven norms of technology. With the energy remaining, let us struggle for the fullfilment of our task five days in advance of schedule and let us support Vietnam with concrete action."*

146-47. *In Peking's main square, Tien An Men, just as in other towns and villages in China, one often comes across small groups of militiamen and women marching. Students, workers, or clerks, they meet in teams outside working hours to learn to march. The soft cotton-soled shoes that they wear in Peking make for a noiseless parade.*

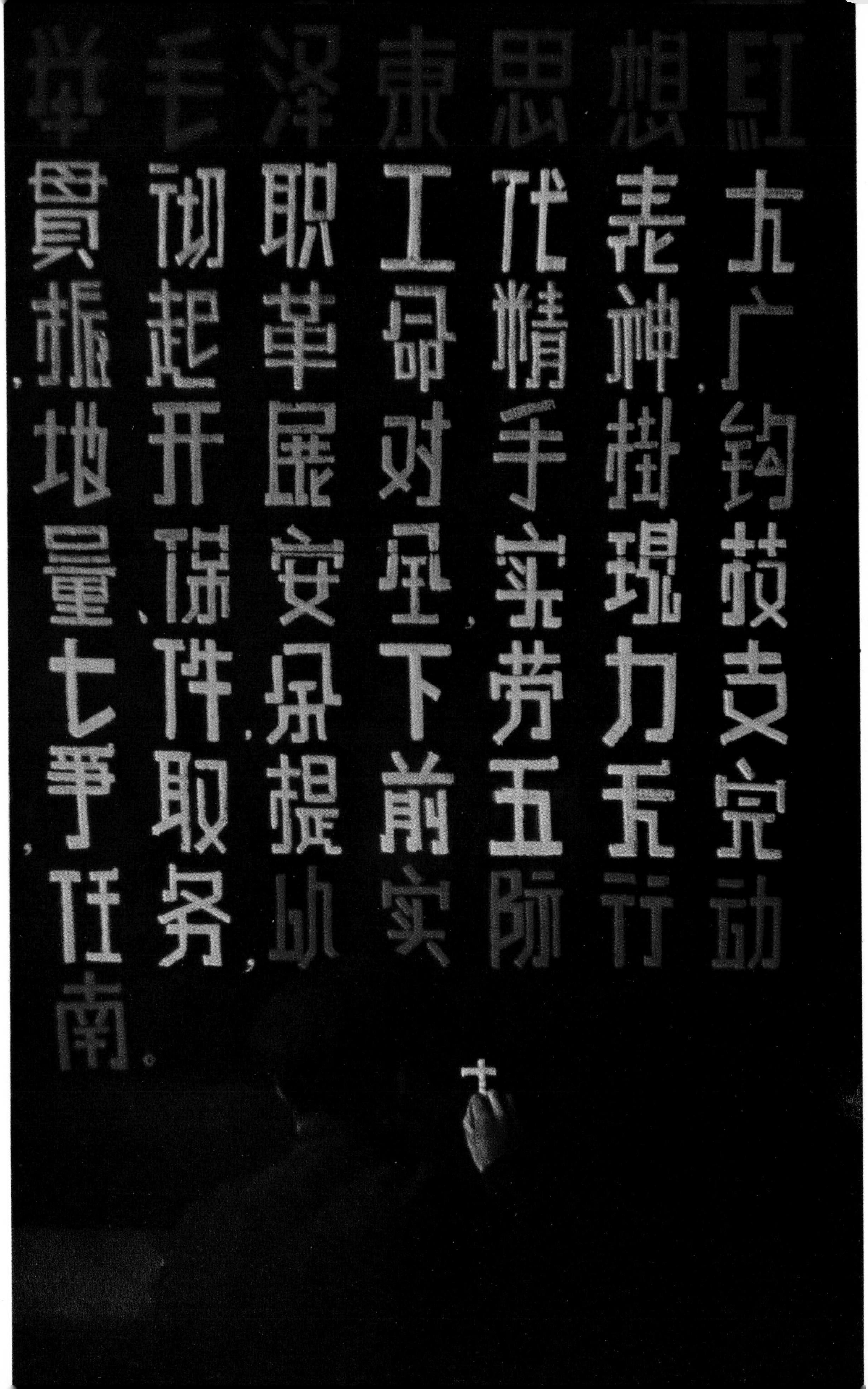

红五广钧菽支党动
想表神挂现力无行
思化精手实劳五际
康工母对坐下前实
泽职革展安朵提动
毛彻起开保件取务
举贯振地量七争任南

148. *Nyerere, President of Tanzania, arrives on a state visit to Peking. Between Chou En-lai and Liu Shao-chi, he reviews the twin rows of the traditional welcoming parade. The car, a "Red Flag," is of Chinese manufacture. There are as yet only about ten of them in existence.*

149. *This mass demonstration on Vietnam was preceded by two days of huge parades. Rallies are always accompanied by speeches punctuated by slogans, such as this one: "We are 700 million united as one man."*

150-51. *The new Peking stadium was built in 1959 for the tenth anniversary of the Revolution. It is used for political demonstrations as well as sporting events. In spite of the rain, 100,000 are gathered here to protest American intervention in the Dominican Republic.*

152-53. *Mass demonstrations always take place in perfect order. The leaders of each team have pieces of paper in their hands bearing the slogans which they get the demonstrators to chant in unison. Factories, offices, and the university send a certain number of "volunteers," varying with the importance of the demonstration.*

154-55. *The famous Buddhist caves of Lungmen (eighth and ninth centuries) in the center of China are no longer a place for religious pilgrimage. Young Pioneers, in their red scarves, and peasants are brought here by the thousands to learn about the ancient civilization of their country.*

156. *Pupils' pails and towels in the corner of a secondary school dormitory. This poverty is not only dictated by economic circumstances; it is part of the educational discipline imposed upon young Chinese, who are constantly being reminded of the hard life of the young Mao.*

157. *In Harbin, in the north, four female students spend their afternoon on the banks of the Sungari, a tributary of the Amur. They still wear pigtails, but there is a growing trend amongst youngsters in favor of short hair. "It takes us too long to plait them every morning," they say.*

158. *At the factory gate, female workers fall into teams. Here they are discussing the news from Vietnam. On other days they read passages from Mao. Frequently they also discuss improved methods in the workshop. Chinese economists claim these meetings contribute to increase productivity.*

159. *Twenty-two-year-old Chiung-hua was awarded a diploma from the Metallurgical Institute of Shanghai two years ago. Now she is a technician at the ball-bearing factory at Kunming, at the other end of China. She lives in a dormitory like the other unmarried workers and administrators in the factory. She has fifteen days vacation a year, which she uses to visit her family.*

160. *It is a southern climate in Canton. Boys and girls, both wearing pants, go for a walk on Sundays in the city's large park. But the short hair of some, the square- or floral-patterned blouses of others, and the boys' ties already show some attempt at sartorial elegance and individuality.*

161. *Kao Mei-tsun, a student at the Peking Petroleum Institute, has fixed Stalin's portrait on the wall of her dormitory. She reckons that he does not deserve "the slanders spread about him by the modern revisionists." All students wear a distinctive enamel insignia of their Institute.*

162. *Such a view of two sweethearts court-
ing in a train is extremely rare. Traditionally the Chinese are very reserved about
displaying their emotions in public. What
we would call puritanism is simply considered prudence in the East.*

163. *The harsh expressions on the faces of
the founders of the Revolution (Liu Shao-
chi, Sun Yat-sen, and Mao Tse-tung) are a
reminder of need to preserve a pure and
austere way of life.*

164. *A foreman from textile factory No. 2 in Peking marries a girl from the south who is in his team. Their workmates have organized a reception being held in the evening classroom. They have drawn the traditional sign of joint happiness on the wall, as well as the inscription: "May this happy union between north and south increase production day and night." The new constitution abolished the old feudal system of forced marriages. Traditional wedding and funeral ceremonies were notorious in old China for ruining families. This is the reason given by the régime for trying to discourage them.*

165. *Once Picasso's dove of peace adorned the retired workers' home in Shenyang (formerly Mukden). Today it is no longer to be seen. China resigned from the World Peace Council because of its "revisionist tendencies."*

166-67. *A divorce court in Peking. The husband wants a divorce because the wife beats the daughter of his first marriage and because she does not keep their home tidy. She replies that she also beats their own child, that he spends all his money outside the home, and that he loves another woman. The members of the court, whose offices (chairman, deputies, and secretary) are described in front of them, refuse a divorce. They advise the couple go on living together and make an effort to get on better. Although divorce is officially recognized in law, the authorities try to restrict it as inimical to the social order.*

166

168. *At Peking University in 1957, the students could dance on Saturday nights. Today dancing in pairs, Western-style, is discouraged as a sign of decadence. Girls are also advised not to marry until after the age of twenty-five and men not until after thirty. It appears that this is one method, among others, of holding down the growth in population. Also the régime hopes to get in this way more study and work out of the young people.*

169. *New elegance in Shanghai. This young glamour-girl has even put on lipstick to be photographed by her fiancé. She is posing in front of a building in a public park which was formerly the property of an extremely wealthy Shanghai businessman. The authorities are proud that feminine stylishness bears witness to an improvement in the standard of living, but at the same time are concerned lest it be a sign of a growing revisionist mentality.*

170-71. *In Peking's zoo, young people do not discuss only productivity or Marxist-Leninism. At the beginning of the Revolution, the campaign of the "five loves," to replace "bourgeois love," was launched: namely, "love of country," "love of the people," "love of work," "love of science," and "love of public property."*

172. *The Chinese New Year in Canton is the occasion for the "Festival of Flowers." This young peasant couple has come from the outskirts to sell the commune's dahlias and marigolds.*

173. *At the end of a reception Chairman Mao Tse-tung drinks to the health of his guests with* maotai, *a rice alcohol. Always dressed in a plain Chinese tunic, he rarely appears in public, but when he does, it is without ceremony or a bodyguard. Mao's two brothers and his first wife were killed during the Revolution. His son fell in the Korean War. He once declared that he found it abnormal that death had thus spared him; it did not seem to want him.*

171

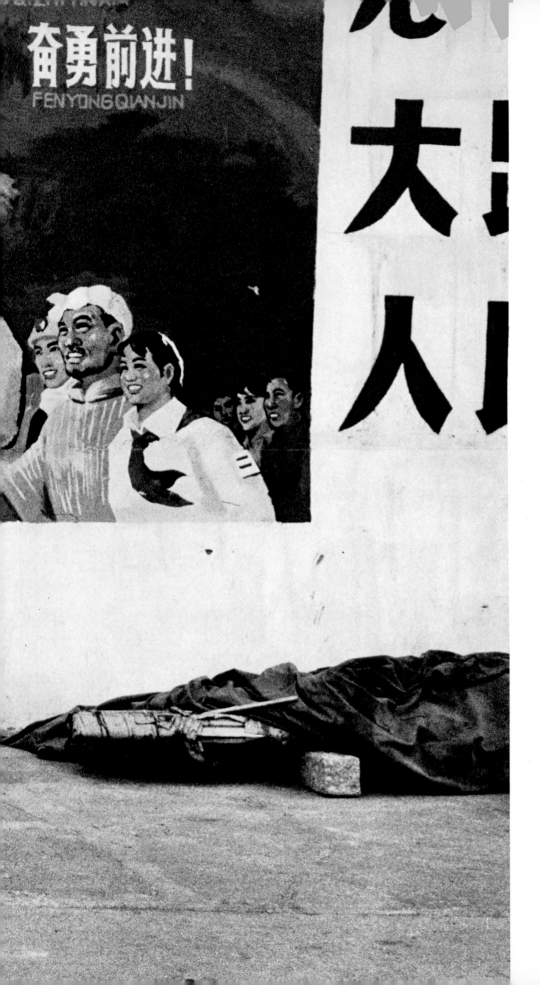

奋勇前进!
FENYONG QIANJIN

174-75. *On posters, everyone moves symbolically leftward. The people are represented here by the worker, the peasant woman, the soldier, the scientist, and the teacher, followed by representatives of the national minorities and the Young Pioneers. They are all marching "beneath the flag of Mao Tse-tung's thought." The photograph was taken in Shanghai's dockland.*

175

176. *In a southern factory, a worker is drawing planes (one of them a U-2). Underneath is the inscription: "Here are the planes used by the bandit Chiang Kai-shek and the American imperialists."*

177. *In Kuelin, in the south, a handwritten notice outside the People's Court announces a death sentence. The condemned man, a teacher, was executed for having raped some of his young pupils. The régime is ruthless in its dealings with this type of crime, which was a scourge of old China. For the translation of the notice, see page 216.*

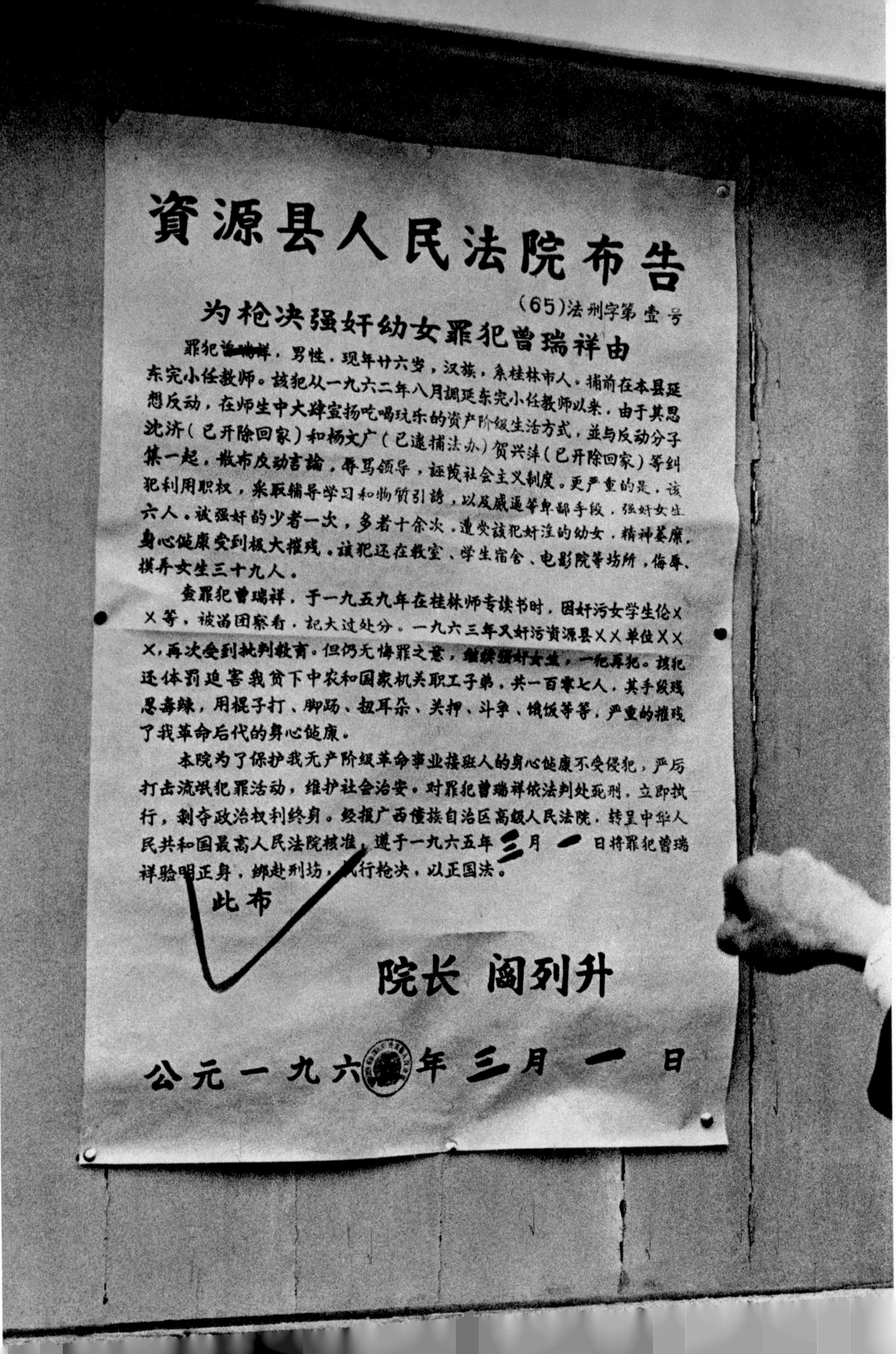

资源县人民法院布告

（65）法刑字第 壹 号

为枪决强奸幼女罪犯曾瑞祥由

罪犯曾瑞祥，男性，现年廿六岁，汉族，系桂林市人。捕前在本县延东完小任教师。该犯从一九六二年八月调延东完小任教师以来，由于其思想反动，在师生中大肆宣扬吃喝玩乐的资产阶级生活方式，并与反动分子沈济（已开除回家）和杨文广（已逮捕法办）贺兴泽（已开除回家）等纠集一起，散布反动言论，辱骂领导，诬蔑社会主义制度。更严重的是，该犯利用职权，采取辅导学习和物质引诱，以及威逼等卑鄙手段，强奸女生六人。该强奸的少者一次，多者十余次。遭受该犯奸淫的幼女，精神萎靡，身心健康受到极大摧残。该犯还在教室、学生宿舍、电影院等场所，侮辱、摸弄女生三十九人。

查罪犯曾瑞祥，于一九五九年在桂林师专读书时，因奸污女学生伦××等，被荷团察看，记大过处分。一九六三年又奸污资源县××单位××，再次受到批判教育。但仍无悔罪之意，继续强奸女生，一犯再犯。该犯还体罚迫害我贫下中农和国家机关职工子弟，共一百零七人，其手段残忍毒辣，用棍子打、脚踢、扭耳朵、关押、斗争、饿饭等等，严重的摧残了我革命后代的身心健康。

本院为了保护我无产阶级革命事业接班人的身心健康不受侵犯，严厉打击流氓犯罪活动，维护社会治安。对罪犯曾瑞祥依法判处死刑，立即执行，剥夺政治权利终身。经报广西僮族自治区高级人民法院，转呈中华人民共和国最高人民法院核准，遂于一九六五年三月一日将罪犯曾瑞祥验明正身，绑赴刑场，执行枪决，以正国法。

　　　　此布

院长　阎列升

公元一九六〇年三月一日

团 结 紧 张　严 肃 活 泼

UNITE ACTIVITE　SEVERITE VIVACITE

178. *May 1 in Peking. Stalin still forms part of the Marxist-Leninist pantheon, together with Marx, Engels, and Lenin.*

179. *A French class in Sian in the heart of China. The teacher, appointed as a result of the cultural agreement which followed French recognition of China, is a young Frenchman. When questioned, the pupils said: "We are learning French in order to serve our country wherever we are needed. We hope it will be in Africa." On the wall is one of the basic slogans, the "Eight's," so called because it consists of eight characters.*

179

180 (above). The customary cups of tea await the visit of a delegation in the reception room of machine-tool factory No. 1 in the new industrial suburb of Peking. The portraits are: Marx, Engels, Lenin and Stalin.

180 (below). Extremely proud of his uniform and stars, an officer poses at the photographer's. A month later came the decision to abolish insignia of rank in the Chinese army. The régime is determined to combat any recrudescence of class spirit.

181. Mao Tse-tung himself told the journalist Edgar Snow: "Some people blame the Chinese people for falling, to some extent, into the cult of personality. There may be some grounds for thinking this. But isn't one entitled to believe that Mr. Krushchev was dismissed because he had no cult of personality at all?"

182-83. Some years ago, in 1957, the pupil-sculptors at the Peking Fine Arts School worked from nude models and in a style inspired by Russian socialist realism. Now they are sent to the communes and factories to use workers and peasants as models. "Art must reflect life."

预防呼吸道传染病

184. *In the art schools, traditional painting is still taught, but the watchword is: "Art in the service of the people."*

185. *Naïve pop art for public hygiene. "Let us prevent contagious diseases of the respiratory system."*

186-87. *A bust of Chairman Mao is a compulsory exercise for students in sculpture.*

188-89. *"The Detachment of Red Women" eis the title of this new revolutionary-styl ballet which tells of an episode in the underground struggle on Hainan Island. Another ballet, inspired by the Vietnam war, is called "Anger in the Coconut Groves." The Peking Opera has also abandoned its traditional style in order to be "closer to life" and to serve revolutionary propaganda.*

190-91. *This is Lei Feng, presented as a hero to Chinese young people. An obliging and obedient soldier, he was killed in a truck accident. The children call him "Uncle Feng." A movie is being shown throughout the entire country illustrating his exemplary life—a life which, according to the Party, was illuminated by daily readings from Mao Tse-tung, as if by a sun.*

192. *This fresco, painted on a village wall, represents the three banners, the main theme of the new, popular official art. They symbolize, in order, the General Line of the Party, the Great Leap Forward, and the People's Communes.*

193. *Political and hygienic advice share the canteen wall in this steel mill. The inscriptions read: "Let us make the Revolution and let us read the works of Chairman Mao throughout our lives." "Never eat spoiled food." "Girls, trim your too long pigtails to avoid accidents."*

194-95. *The army takes part in public-works programs. Here, near Nanning, an infantry unit is widening the road which leads to North Vietnam. From his Long March, Mao has always kept the idea that the army must be at the center of the Revolution and that the soldier must be a worker, mingling with the people.*

196-97. *Somewhere on the immense plateau of Inner Mongolia a local folk-group, accompanied by a traditional orchestra, interprets a revolutionary theme.*

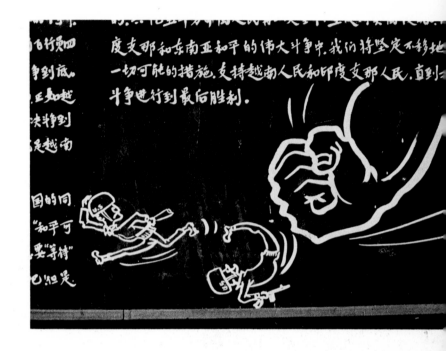

198. *For every problem of life and labor, a text from Mao provides the correct solution. This one says: "Hard work is like a heavy load placed before us, challenging us to shoulder it. Some people choose the light loads and leave the heavy ones to others. This is not the correct attitude." This quotation from Mao dates from the struggle against the Japanese. This group of soldiers, returning from roadbuilding, placed the sign near a heap of stones waiting to be loaded.*

199. *"We will adopt all measures within our power to support the Vietnamese people until their final victory." Today, Vietnam is the main theme of meetings and propaganda.*

200-201. *"Everyone a soldier." "The army and the people are an ocean in which the invader must drown." Thus sayeth Mao. The people's militia is the people in arms and every Chinese must belong to it. But equipment is rough and ready. There is no ammunition for target practice carried out with weapons of World War II vintage. No pigtails for militiagirls.*

202. *Students must devote one day a week to manual work in the public interest. Future cadres, seen here on a construction site, will know what a coolie's pole is.*

203. *At the other end of the scale, there are attempts to arouse the political and cultural awareness of the workers. These are listening to a lecture on Marxist-Leninism.*

204-05. *An open-air mime drama. In a parade in support of Vietnam, amateur actors take off the American spy-pilot and Uncle Sam, both caught up in the chains of Vietnamese fighters. Westerners are always played and drawn with long noses.*

The American John Kenneth Galbraith has written: "Wealth is the relentless enemy of under-standing... as with individuals, so with nations." In our part of the world, as the same professor puts it, "More people die from overeating than from undernourishment." Isn't it difficult thus for us to judge in its real perspective a choice involving "famine" as the Asians know it and "free-dom" as we know it?

In countries like our own, which have passed beyond a certain level of economic development and which have taken centuries to organize and modernize, the free-enterprise system, with its spirit of competition, is an obvious instrument of material progress and cultural enrichment for the majority. But, when applied to countries where most of the population still lives far below this level, is not the same system producing the opposite reaction which leads to social disintegration, chaos, and the law of the jungle? In a poor society where there is no security and no hope, man can survive only through complete selfishness and his most inhuman instincts reappear.

This was the situation in China fifteen years ago. Since Sun Yat-sen's revolution in 1911, liberalism had forty years to show its stuff. In spite of some genuine efforts, the chaos only increased, and, in 1949, China was a country where 80 per cent of the population was illiterate, in which there was barely one doctor to every 30,000 persons, no industry to speak of, and where 25,000 corpses were picked up annually in the streets of Shanghai. That an alternate like Maoist Communism would be tried was inevitable.

Leaving China for one of the neighboring countries, one cannot fail to be struck by the change in the expression and bearing of the people. Cleanliness, order, and collective discipline give the Chinese, even the poorest, a self-respect which contrasts with the despondency seen elsewhere in Asia. The clean streets, the children going to school, the peasants learning to read, the sick being cared for, the absence of theft and prostitution, the trains arriving on time, the factories being built—all these are cause for Chinese pride as well as for meaningful life and hope.

Of course there are grounds for apprehension lest other temptations be nurtured in the minds of leaders who can utilize the unity and the militancy of such a gigantic mass of people. To this the country's leaders, who are frequently accused of aggressive aims, reply that they have legitimate reasons for believing that China is threatened.

And this fierce pressure, which tends to produce a uniform and obedient mass—how long is the leadership going to exert it? Indeed, do they want to? Or are the results themselves, arrived at thanks to this obstinacy, going to provoke certain changes?

Leaving China, a Westerner can't help thinking: this is a world where life would be impossible. Such regimentation, depersonalization, conformity, and puritanism are unbearable for a Westerner. But present-day China is not a country for immigrants or tourists. She is not interested in pleasing the foreigner. Her problem and her pride is to thrust into the twentieth century 700 million people born in misery. Her pertinacity is to remain revolutionary to the end.

from the writings of mao tse-tung

The Chinese people are told to read the works of Mao Tse-tung every day. The worker, the peasant, the soldier, the engineer, the professor, the artist—each is supposed to look into Mao Tse-tung's writings for moral and philosophical guidance and, for that matter, answers to daily problems. The slogan is, "Always follow the teachings of President Mao." Mao's works, so far published in four volumes, have been assembled into a loosely organized collection of articles, letters, and speeches dating from 1932 to 1957, covering the history of the Chinese Communist Party along with comments on ethics, morals, and ideology. There are also personal recollections. The following quotations are drawn from these volumes.

A revolution is not the same as inviting people to dinner, or writing an essay, or painting a picture, or doing fancy needlework; it cannot be anything so refined, so calm and gentle, or so mild, kind and courteous, restrained and magnanimous. A revolution is ... an act of violence whereby one class overthrows another. 1927 ● *When human society advances to the point where classes and states are eliminated, there will no longer be any wars, whether revolutionary or counter-revolutionary, just or unjust, and that will be an era of lasting peace for mankind. Our study of the laws of revolutionary war starts from our will to eliminate all wars—this is the dividing line between us Communists and all exploiting classes.* 1936 ● *Wars in history can be divided into two kinds, just and unjust. All progressive wars are just and all wars impeding progress are unjust. We Communists are opposed to all unjust wars that impede progress, but we are not opposed to progressive, just wars.* 1938 ● *I hold that it is bad, as far as we are concerned, if a person, a political party, an army, or a school is not attacked by the enemy. For in that case, it would mean that we have sunk to the level of the enemy. It is good if we are attacked by the enemy, since it proves that we have drawn a clear line of demarcation between the enemy and ourselves. It is still better if the enemy attacks us wildly and paints us utterly black and without a single virtue, since it demonstrates that we have not only drawn a clear line of demarcation between the enemy and ourselves, but achieved a great deal in our work.* 1939 ● *Revolutionary art and literature are part of the entire cause of the Revolution, they are its cogs and screws; though in comparison with certain other parts they may be less important and less urgent and occupy only a secondary position, yet they are, as cogs and screws, indispensable to the whole machine, and form an indispensable part of the entire cause of the Revolution. If we had no art and literature even in the broadest and most general sense, then the revolu-*

tionary movement could not be carried on to victory. ... There is in reality no such thing as art for art's sake, art which stands above classes or art which runs parallel to or remains independent of politics. 1942 ● *Imperialist aggression shattered the fond dreams of the Chinese about learning from the West. It was very odd—why were the teachers always committing aggression against their pupil? The Chinese learned a good deal from the West, but they could not make it work and were never able to realize their ideals. Their repeated struggles, including such a country-wide movement as the Revolution of 1911, all ended in failure. Day by day, conditions in the country got worse, and life was made impossible. Doubts arose, increased, and deepened.* 1949 ● *The atom bomb is a paper tiger which the U.S. reactionaries use to scare people. It looks terrible, but in fact it isn't. Of course the atom bomb is a weapon of mass slaughter, but the outcome of a war is decided by the people, not by one or two types of weapons.* 1949 ● *All reactionaries are paper tigers. In appearance, the reactionaries are terrifying, but in reality they are not so powerful. From a long-term point of view, it is not the reactionaries, but the people who are really powerful. ... Speaking of U.S. imperialism, people seem to feel it is terrifically strong. ... But it will be proved that the U.S. reactionaries, like all reactionaries in history, do not have much strength. ... The reason is simply this: the reactionaries represent reaction; we represent progress.* 1949 ● *As for love of mankind, there has been no such all-embracing love since the human race was divided into classes. The ruling classes have preached universal love. Confucius advocated it, as did Tolstoy. But no one has ever been able to practice it because it cannot be attained in a class society. A true love of mankind is attainable, but only in the future when class distinctions will have been eliminated throughout the world. Classes serve to divide society; when classes are eliminated, society will be united again. At that time, the love of mankind will flourish but it cannot flourish now. Today we cannot love the fascists nor can we love our enemies. We cannot love all that is evil and ugly in society. It is our objective to eliminate all these evils. The people know that. Cannot our writers and artists understand it?* 1950 ● *Given specific conditions, the two aspects of a contradiction invariably turn into their respective opposites as a result of the struggle between them. The present situation in which the United States controls a majority in the United Nations and dominates many parts of the world is a transient one, which will eventually be changed. China's situation as a poor country denied her rights in international affairs will also be changed—a poor country will be changed into a rich country, a country denied her rights into a country enjoying her rights—a transformation of things into their opposites.* 1957 ● *Any attempt to deal with ideological matters or questions involving right and wrong, by administrative orders or coercive measures, will not only be ineffective but harmful. We cannot abolish religion by administrative orders; nor can we force people not to believe in it. We cannot compel people to give up idealism any more than we can force them to believe in Marxism. In settling matters of an ideological nature or controversial issues among the people, we can only use democratic methods, methods of discussion, of criticism, of persuasion and education, not coercive, high-handed methods. ... What should our policy be towards non-Marxist ideas?—As far as unmistakable counter-revolutionaries and wreckers of the socialist cause are concerned, the matter is easy: we simply deprive them of their freedom of speech. But it is quite a different matter when we are faced with incorrect ideas among the people. Will it do to ban such ideas and give them no opportunity to express themselves? Certainly not. It is not only futile but very harmful to use crude and summary methods to deal with ideological questions among the people, with questions relating to the spiritual life of man. You may ban the expression of wrong ideas, but the ideas will still be there. On the other hand, correct ideas, if pampered in hot-houses without being exposed to the elements or immunized from disease, will not win out against wrong ones. That is why it is only by employing methods of discussion, criticism, and reasoning that we can really foster correct ideas, overcome wrong ideas, and really settle issues.* 1957 ● *We stand resolutely for peace and oppose war. But if the imperialists insist on unleashing another war, we should not be afraid of it. Our attitude on this question is the same as our attitude towards all disturbance: firstly we are against it; secondly, we are not afraid of it.* 1957 ● *China's 600 million people are first of all poor, and secondly, "blank." This may seem like a bad thing, but it is really a good thing. Poor people want change, want to do things, want revolution. A clean sheet of paper has no blotches and the newest and most beautiful words can be written on it, the newest and most beautiful pictures can be painted on it.* 1958 ● *The intellectual should comport himself in front of the people as humbly as an ox in front of a child. One must wash the spirit in the same way one washes one's face every morning.* ● *Learning is like rowing a boat against stream; if one stops, one goes backwards.* ● *The precepts of the Revolution should be more dear to a Communist than his own life.*

U.S.S.R.

Urumuchi

Sinkiang

Tsinghai

Tibet

NEPAL

Lhassa

Sikang

BUTAN

INDIA

Y

The heavy line represents the author's itin-
erary inside China during his trip of 1965.

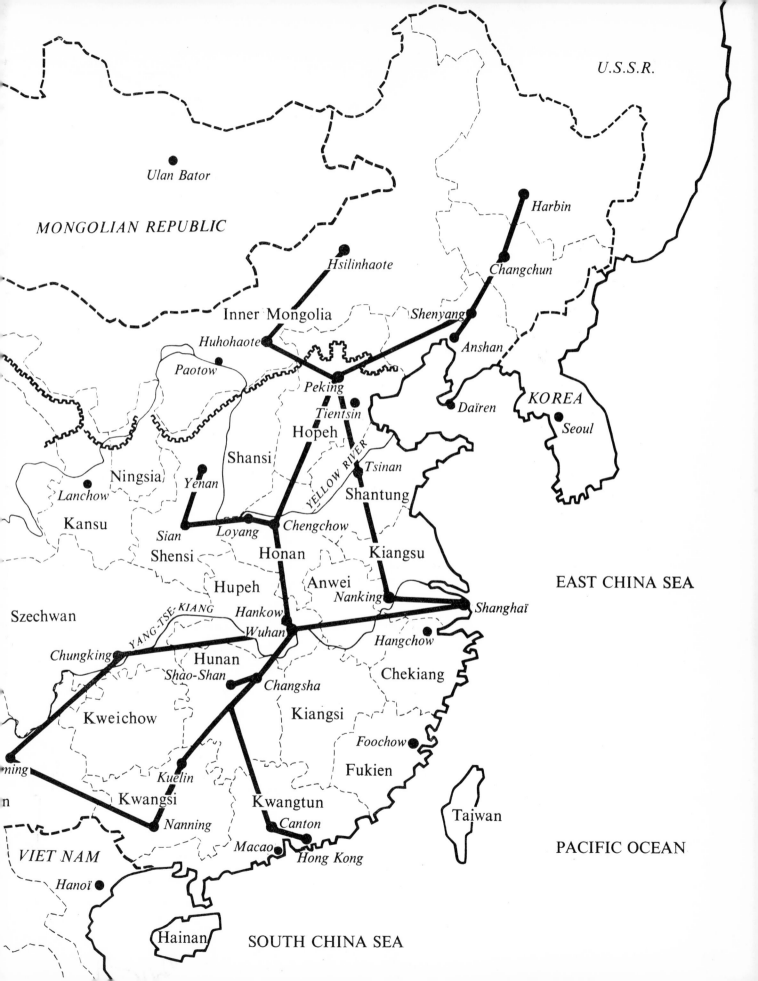

Translation of notice in photograph on page 177:

Verdict of the People's Court of the County
of Tzu-Yuan (65) Criminal sentence No. 1
Death penalty for the criminal Tseng Jui-yang,
accused of rape of minors

The accused, Tseng Jui-yang, male, twenty-six years old and of the Han race, comes from the town of Kueilin. Before his arrest he was a teacher at the primary school of Yen-Tung in this county. Since his appointment in August 1962, the accused, as a consequence of his reactionary ideology, began to propagate amongst his fellow teachers and his pupils the example of a dissipated and bourgeois manner of living. Moreover, aided and abetted by reactionary elements such as Shen Chi (already expelled and sent home), Yang Wen-kuang (already arrested and judged according to the law), and Ho Hsing Ping (already expelled and sent home), etc., he distributed reactionary tracts, insulted the leadership, and slandered the socialist system. Even more serious is the fact that the accused, taking advantage of his position, on the pretext of giving educational advice, using bribes, threats, and other vulgar methods, raped six pupils. The offence was committed from one to ten times, according to the victims. The young pupils whom he raped suffered irreparable harm to their bodies and minds. In addition, the accused indecently assaulted thirty-nine pupils in dormitories, movie theatres, classrooms, and other places. It appears that the accused, Tseng Jui-yang, when he was a student at the teacher's training college in Kueilin in 1959, seduced a fellow student named Lun X. As a punishment, Tseng was placed under the surveillance of the League [the Youth movement] and received a very severe reprimand. In 1963, the accused

once more seduced X from X in the county of Tzu-Yuan and was once more the subject of severe criticism. However, the accused displayed no sign of repentance and continued to rape his pupils. Moreover, the accused inflicted corporal punishment upon 107 pupils, children of our poor and very poor peasants, employees, and state workers. His methods were cruel. He used sticks to beat the children on their heels, he twisted their ears, locked them up, deprived them of food, and so on, thus destroying the moral and physical well-being of our new revolutionary generations.

In order to safeguard the moral and physical well-being of the inheritors of our proletarian revolution, in order to punish severely the activites of this criminal thug, and in order to protect the structure of society, this court has, according to the law, sentenced the accused, Tseng Jui-yang, to death (the sentence to be carried out at once) and has ordered the removal for life of his political rights. This sentence was approved by the Supreme People's Court of the People's Republic of China, to which it was transmitted by the People's Court of the autonomous region of Chung in Kwangsi province. This court, in enforcing the above verdict, and in order to preserve justice in the country, after having verified the identity of the accused, Tseng Jui-yang, and after having bound him and led him to the place of execution, carried out the sentence by shooting on March 1, 1965.

For Information, the President of the Court, Yen Lieh-sheng

March 1, 1965 A.D.

壯　妥　特　攘　舊　連　論　散　田　低
工　貌　鴃　豫　老　淩　勉　我　禪
徘　頻　躍　　少　摩　其　藝　主
徊　妍　超　且　異　絳　逍　祗　云
瞻　笑　驤　且　糧　霄　遙　植　亭
　　季　驤　康　　　　桂　稅
　　　　誅　嫡　御　欣　省　稅
陋　矢　斬　後　　讀　奏　　閒
　　　賊　嗣　續　績　觀　門